Baby
SHOWERS

Jennifer Adams

Gibbs Smith, Publisher
Salt Lake City

First Edition
10 09 08 07 06 5 4 3 2

Published by
Gibbs Smith, Publisher
P.O. Box 667
Layton, Utah 84041

Orders: 1.800.748.5439
www.gibbs-smith.com

Designed by Dawn DeVries Sokol
Cover artwork © CSAimages.com
Printed and bound in China

Library of Congress Cataloging-in-Publication Data

Adams, Jennifer.
  Baby showers / Jennifer Adams.— 1st ed.
      p. cm.
  ISBN 1-58685-774-6
  1. Showers (Parties) 2. Infants. I. Title.

GV1472.7.S5A313 2006
793.2—dc22

2005025797

DEDICATION

For my mother,
Linda Hunter Adams

◦ Contents ◦

Acknowledgments

Thank you to Alison Koritz for hosting so many showers over the years. Thanks also to Dayna Shoell, Dorothy Capson, Patrice Mealy, Stephanie Black, Kris Russell, Janna DeVore, Shauna Larson, Michelle Knepper, Teresa Hazen, Olga Grillone, and Sheryl Smith for excellent recipes.

Thanks to Suzanne Taylor and Madge Baird for their support and leadership, to Kellie Robles for her friendship and insight, to Dawn DeVries Sokol for creative design and moral support on many projects, and to all my friends at Gibbs Smith, Publisher.

Fondness and thanks to my book group for helping test the recipes included here.

Thanks also go to Charles P. Adams, Linda Hunter Adams, Nathan Adams, Melissa Grillone, Morgan Grillone, and Virgil Grillone for giving me time to write and supporting this book.

INTRODUCTION

Why do women put up with morning sickness, go through the wrenching pains of labor, and commit to a life of permanent worry about their child from the day he or she is born? When it all comes down to it, I think it may just be because of those tiny, adorable little baby shoes. I've never met a woman who could resist the little pink Converse high-tops or the miniature Nikes. Can you?

Seriously, though, there are hard things about being pregnant, and it's easily the biggest commitment a woman will ever make—even bigger than marriage since you can get divorced, but you can't divorce your child! There are so many fun and whimsical elements to having a baby, too, and that is where this book comes in.

Baby showers are to celebrate the fun of it all—the outfits and the teddy bears and those little miniature shoes. They're about decorating the nursery, finding the right bedtime stories, and planning the future. They're a time to join together with family and friends to welcome a new little person into the world.

BABY SHOWER BASICS

A shower is a celebration—a time to "shower" an expectant mother with gifts to express love and congratulations. Throughout history women in many different cultures have gathered to honor a new mother and give her gifts. Following are some baby shower basics to keep in mind when planning a modern-day baby shower.

Showers were traditionally for the firstborn child and were a way to help with the expense of setting up a nursery, including all the clothes, bedding, and other baby items that a new mother would need to have. Currently the thinking for many is that every baby is a cause for celebration, so showers for second or even third babies are much more common.

Be sure to think things through as you plan showers for second and third babies, however. If you throw a second shower for one woman in a group of friends, you are committing to throwing showers for second babies of all the women in that group. You don't want to tire out and taper off so some women get second showers and others do not. A nice compromise for a second baby shower is to treat the mom to lunch at her favorite restaurant or give a group gift instead of having everyone bring a gift. But if you and your friends or family want to give a full-blown shower, then have fun with it!

A good occasion to give a shower for a baby that is not the first baby is for surprise babies that come years later than their siblings—after the parents thought they were through having their family and have given away everything from the crib to the clothing. And it's perfectly appropriate to throw a shower for a family that has had all girls and then has a boy, or vice versa. It's nice to give the mom some items that are especially for her new baby's gender.

◦ WHO GIVES THE SHOWER ◦

Someone close to the mother-to-be should host the shower—a friend, coworker, or aunt, for example. Traditionally mothers and sisters are not supposed to host showers; it seems inappropriate to ask for gifts for a direct family member. Many people have become more lax on this standard; however, proper etiquette leaves hosting to someone other than the immediate family of the expectant mom.

○ WHEN TO HAVE THE SHOWER ○

Four to six weeks before the baby's due date is a typical time to throw a baby shower. As the mom nears the end of her pregnancy, she deserves an opportunity to celebrate. At this point, she is most likely almost finished putting together her nursery and trying to figure out what kinds of things she needs to buy, from pajamas to baby shampoo. After the shower, she'll have a better idea of what she's still missing.

In some religions and cultures, however, it is inappropriate to have the shower before the baby arrives. In these instances, it's nice to plan the shower for six to eight weeks after the baby is born. This gives the mom a chance to recuperate a little and the baby a chance to build up some immunity before being exposed to a large group.

Other women might choose to have the shower after the baby arrives. For example, if the expectant mom has been sick or is on bed rest before the baby comes, it works well to have the shower after the baby arrives. It's also a

nice option if the mom wants to wait to find out the sex of the baby. In any case, showers after the baby is born have the added benefit of allowing the baby to make a guest appearance!

∘ ADOPTED BABIES ∘

Another time you will want to have the baby shower after the baby arrives is when you are holding a baby shower for an adopted child. Adoptions can take months, even years, and adoptive parents often don't know whether an adoption will go through until the very last minute. The arrival of an adopted baby is as much a cause for joy and celebration as the arrival of a baby that comes in any other way. You might want to include a phrase on the invitations such as "celebrating the arrival of" as a hint that the baby is adopted. If the baby is older, you might want to make a note of his or her age as well, so that guests don't bring gifts for newborns. In almost all cases, everyone who is invited to a baby shower will know the mother well enough to realize that she is adopting her baby rather than giving birth, but if there is any question be sure to make it clear beforehand so that no guest inadvertently makes a comment that would be hurtful to the mother or detract from the celebration at hand.

◦ WHERE TO HAVE THE SHOWER ◦

Most showers are given at the host's home, which works well and is a simple and comfortable setting for the party. There are always other venues, of course. If you are having a shower with people from work who live at a distance from each other, you can host the shower in the work conference room or in a central location. Many times people enjoy going to a restaurant for lunch. A backyard, clubhouse, or even the beach or a park can be pleasant places to host a get-together, especially in cases where you are having a large party or where you want to take advantage of nice weather.

◦ WHOM TO INVITE ◦

Work with the expectant mom to create a guest list for the shower. Sometimes it is not as straightforward as it may appear. Remember that many times the mother-to-be is having more than one shower. She might want to include family in one group and friends in another. Often there is overlap; there may be some people—like her mother—that she'd like to include on more than one list, or she may be worried about the cost of asking friends to bring gifts to more than one event. With her help, you can get the right group for the shower. Be sure to have her give you a list of people's addresses well in advance of the shower.

Plan the group's size according to the type of shower you want to give. I've been to showers with as few as six people and as many as forty. It all depends on the kind of party you want to have. I find the most rewarding shower includes about eight people or so; the intimacy of a smaller group is enjoyable and more memorable, and it's nice when the mother-to-be has time to talk with the guests in a comfortable setting. Always work toward putting together a group that makes sense for the shower—one where there is a logical dividing line of who is included, and where the people know each other and will enjoy each other's company. Be careful not to leave anyone out who will be hurt by not being included.

◦ COUPLES SHOWERS ◦

Couples showers have become somewhat popular. They especially make sense when there is a group of couples who are friends, where the boyfriends and husbands know each other and get along independently of their girlfriends and wives. This kind of shower will have a very different feel from a traditional baby shower. I'd suggest that everyone go out to dinner or have a backyard barbeque along with some activities—anything from a marshmallow roast to board games and cards. I once went to a traditionally planned shower where the men were invited. While the women "oohed" and "ahhed" over baby blankets and fringed burp cloths, the men milled around uncomfortably or surreptitiously read a cast-aside *TV Guide.* Personally, I recommend sticking to a community of women in most cases for celebrating the arrival of an infant. But there are definitely certain groups of friends for which a couples shower would be rewarding.

◦ PLAN AHEAD ◦

Plan ahead the kind of shower you want to give and who you want to include. Once you select a theme, ideas will begin to unfold, from the number of people you want to invite, to the food you want to serve, to the kind of invitations to select. Planning in advance helps things go much more smoothly. Plan down to the details ahead of time and organize yourself with idea lists, shopping lists, and checklists.

Another thing that will make things simpler is if you limit the number of people who help with the shower. Planning the event with a close friend is a great idea and you can have a lot of fun together. However, be careful not to get too many people involved or else things may become disorganized. In many cases, especially with work showers, everyone will offer to help. Unless you want your shower to feel like a mismatched potluck, it's best to thank people graciously, but let them know you've got things covered. Otherwise, you will likely have people who are assigned food (a) come late, (b) come without their food made and want to use your kitchen to prepare it at the last minute, or (c) come with the wrong food that clashes with the menu you've planned. I've had all three happen.

∘ BE FLEXIBLE ∘

Be flexible in dealing with the simple setbacks that will almost assuredly arise the day of the shower. Remember that even with the best-planned event things can go awry, whether the quiche you wanted to serve doesn't set or someone you counted on for help doesn't show up. Move quickly to Plan B, and don't let the upset ruin the event.

Of course it's easier to relax and enjoy a party if there are no surprises, and the better you plan ahead of time, the less likely it is that there will be surprises. However, on the day of the shower, let yourself go with the flow. Remember, if you can relax and have a good time, then so can your guests. And having a good time is the goal.

◦ MAKE A TIMELINE ◦

It helps to make a master plan and timeline of what you want to accomplish. Most of your planning will be done six to eight weeks prior to the event. You can use the timeline that follows to help you. In addition, plan ahead when buying your gift and selecting party favors.

Buy your gift for the shower early and stash it away; then you can wrap it when the day of the shower approaches. One reason to do this is that you can spread the cost of the shower out over several months. Another reason is that there is a danger of waiting until the last minute to buy the gift that you'll be so overwhelmed with other food and decorating preparations that you may not have time to savor choosing the perfect present. You'll also want to plan well in advance if your gift is hand-made, such as a quilt or a baby book.

Planning ahead holds true for the party favors as well. I've given showers where I didn't have favors because I waited until the last day to get them, and by that time I was out of time, energy, or money. While it's perfectly fine to give a shower without favors, it's a nice touch to have them and not much trouble if you plan for them in advance. If you are giving favors that can be made or bought ahead of time, buy them a month before and put them away for the shower.

TIMELINE

*2 months before
the shower
(not before the
baby's due date)*

Talk to the expectant mother
    about hosting a shower.
Pick a date and location.
Determine the guest list.

*6 weeks before
the shower*

Plan the menu and decorations.
Buy or make the invitations.

*4 weeks before
the shower*

Buy your gift.
Buy party favors.

*3–4 weeks before
the shower*

Send out invitations.
Check on your linens,
    serving dishes, and so on.

2 weeks before the shower	Deep clean your house and/or
	    yard if hosting at home.
	Order flowers.
	Buy nonperishable food
	    for the menu.
	Buy or make other decorations.

2–3 days before the shower	Do final cleaning.

The day before or the day of the shower	Buy perishable favors. Buy perishable food for the menu. Make the food. Set up the decorations. Pick up the flowers.

THEMES

Organizing a baby shower by theme gives you a framework in which to plan. Once you determine a theme, ideas for invitations, games, decorations, and food begin to emerge. A theme also makes your event feel like a cohesive whole. There are many different themes you can choose from. Be creative. Some favorites are outlined in this chapter.

○ SHOWERS FOR A BABY GIRL ○

Pink, pink, pink! As stereotypical as it sounds, it's so much fun to go wild with pink for a baby shower for a girl. You can use pale pink, hot pink, or a combination of both. Use flowers, stripes, polka dots, or plaids—or mix and match them. Use pink in any combination for the tablecloth, invitations, decorations, and even the frosting on the cake or the icing on the cookies.

Decorate with bunches of pink balloons and arrange pink and white flowers for centerpieces. If you send out invitations announcing a shower for a baby girl, your guest of honor will usually receive a lot of pink outfits and sweet little dresses. (If the mom-to-be would like more variety in the presents, it's better not to announce the shower is for a girl.)

Pink also works well if you want to develop a princess or tea-party theme for your shower.

○ SHOWERS FOR A BABY BOY ○

As with a shower for a baby girl, it's easy to organize a shower for a baby boy around a simple color theme. Light blue and white work well as a color combination; red and navy are fun, too.

Other fun themes for a baby boy shower include trains, cars and trucks, or a sandbox. For a shower with a train theme, you can set up a toy train as your center-piece, or focus around a children's book about trains (such as *The Polar Express* or *The Little Engine That Could).* Incorporate this theme into your invitations as well. For a car-and-truck shower, send out an invitation featuring an illustrated car or truck. Decorate your serving table with Tonka trucks and adorn the room with construction and traffic signs that you make out of poster board, such as "men at work," "yield," "railroad crossing," and "stop." For a beach or sandbox theme, gifts might include children's picture books that feature the beach, a swimming suit, a beach towel, a beach ball, baby sunglasses and sunblock, or toys that are useful for digging in the sandbox, like a bucket and plastic shovel. Make the centerpiece for your serving table a fishbowl with live goldfish and give shower favors in mini tin buckets.

WE'RE-WAITING-TO-FIND-OUT
◦ BABY SHOWER ◦

A woman I knew had an ultrasound that told her she was having a baby girl. She and her husband painted the nursery pink, got pink floral bedding, and had all of their showers for a girl. Imagine their surprise when their son was born! That's just one reason it's sometimes a good

idea to have a non-gender-specific shower. Aside from that, many women like to wait until their delivery day to find out the sex of their baby. And, as mentioned previously, non-gender-specific showers often yield more variety in the presents received.

There are many fun color schemes that accommodate either a baby boy or girl. Deck out your house in pale yellow and white or in a combination of aqua and lavender. Many people also like to combine pink and light blue as the colors for this type of shower.

A classic Winnie the Pooh shower is a fun theme for either a girl or boy baby. Decorate with classic Pooh plush toys and hardbound copies of the *Winnie the Pooh* books by A. A. Milne. I always advocate classic Winnie the Pooh over the Disney version; it is more upscale, classic, and less commercialized.

Another easy way to decorate is with wooden alphabet blocks. They make a fun centerpiece for your buffet table and can be featured on your invitations.

○ RUBBER-DUCKY BATH-TIME SHOWER ○

For a bath-time shower, send invitations that have a rubber ducky printed on them (you can usually find at least one set of this type in the stationery store or you can make them). A more creative—if more elaborate—alternative is to put all the information about the shower on a small flat-panel card and tie it around the neck of an actual rubber ducky. This works well if guests live close by and you can deliver the invitations in person. Or, if you are willing to spend a little extra for postage and mailing boxes, you can stick these invitations in the mail. On the invitations, ask guests to bring gifts related to bath time. Gifts would include a baby bathtub, bath towels, robes, baby shampoo and lotion, bathtub toys, and pajamas for putting baby to bed after a bath.

○ MOON-AND-STARS BEDTIME SHOWER ○

For this shower, send invitations featuring moons and stars and decorate your house with the same. You can make a mobile of stars to hang over your serving table. Gifts for this type of shower theme would include onesies, pajamas, diapers, blankets, decorative pillows, a mobile for the crib, plush toys, and even a book to read at bedtime. Chunky silver magnets in the shape of stars could be given as shower favors.

○ STORY-TIME SHOWER ○

No one disputes the benefits of reading aloud to your baby, and this shower is especially fun if you are a book lover. It's a great way to build up a library for the little one. Make a centerpiece for your table out of favorite children's books. On the invitations, let guests know that this is a story-time shower and ask them to bring their favorite children's book as the gift. Mini books make nice party favors to complement this shower. You could also have a drawing for a favorite children's picture book that you select.

Perfect Gift Books
for STORY-TIME Shower

Chicka Chicka Boom Boom

Frog and Toad Together

Goodnight Moon

Guess How Much I Love You

Love You Forever

Olivia

On the Day You Were Born

The Tale of Peter Rabbit

The Velveteen Rabbit

The Very Hungry Caterpillar

Where the Wild Things Are

Winnie the Pooh

INVITATIONS

Most women who enjoy entertaining savor the task of selecting and sending the invitations to their party. It's a way of looking forward to the event to come. Baby shower invitations are no exception—in fact, choosing or making these invitations will get your creativity flowing and can be a pure pleasure. Baby shower invites encompass some of the best stationery around. This chapter will give you a variety of ideas for choosing or making the perfect invitation.

I am always on the lookout for stationery and invitations that I like. It's fun to browse favorite stationery shops, bookstores, gift shops, and boutiques for cards and papers. When you are shopping for invitations for a baby shower, keep the mother-to-be in mind. By finding invitations that match her taste and sense of style, you'll be on your way to determining the kind of shower you want to give. If you've already picked the theme for your shower, find invitations that reflect that theme.

You can choose cute, smart, sassy, precious, elegant, classic, or contemporary invitations. Buy invitations that are already made and have them imprinted at the stationery store, print them on your home computer, or write them out by hand. Or you can make your own invitations. There are an abundance of card stocks, papers, and vellums in unlimited colors, textures, and patterns to choose from. You can create your invitations using hand-made add-ons designed for use in scrapbooking and handmade cards. Create just the look you want by adding a tiny paper duck, umbrella, bottle, rattle, or daisy to a long narrow piece of card stock, or by printing on a velum overlay and then placing the sheet over a polka-dot background. Ribbons of different thicknesses can be glued to the front of cards to add a tactile quality to your invitation. Or affix a small, flat metal icon, such as a baby bootie or letters to spell out "baby" or "ABC."

Letterpress invitations are another option to keep in mind. Although they can be somewhat more expensive than regular invitations, almost nothing speaks of style the way letterpress printing can. Depending on the type of design you choose, the invitations can be whimsical, formal, modern, or anything in between; no matter what the style, letterpress printing is exquisite.

Don't forget to pay attention to the envelopes for your shower invitations. Boxed invitations come with envelopes that match the cards. If you are making your invitations, you can use opaque vellum envelopes to highlight the card inside or choose envelopes with a grommet and string wraparound enclosure on the back. You can include a hint of the card's design on the envelope, even if it is something as simple as adding a matching sticker or using a pen with an ink that matches the invitation colors.

◦ STAMPS ◦

Everyone enjoys getting something in the mail besides bills, and in almost all cases you should mail your shower invitations rather than hand deliver them. Avoid the urge to stick them in your coworker's in-box or interoffice mail. An invitation in the mail with a handwritten address (not a computer-printed sticker) says that thought and time are going in to planning the party and that it is going to be something special.

Buy stamps that match your invitations in feeling or design. You can buy anything from love stamps to dinosaur stamps depending on the theme of your shower. A nice idea is to go to www.photostamps.com. Here you can submit a photo that is made into an actual printed stamp that is approved by the U.S. Postal Service. This is a nice idea if you are giving a shower after the baby is born. Get a photo of the newborn and scan it or have the parents send you a photo as an email attachment, and then transform the photo of baby into a stamp for the invitations.

◦ INVITATION RESOURCES ◦

Selecting your baby shower invitations can be one of the creative highlights of the shower. Following is a list of favorite stationery lines to look for. Some of these invitations and papers can be purchased online. In most cases, the website will direct you to the store nearest you that carries the line of stationery you are interested in.

STATIONERY RESOURCES

Lines to look for at your favorite stationery store:

- Bebe
- Crane
- Lulu

- Meri Meri
- Pepperpot
- William Arthur

Other stationery lines and retail stores:

Anna Griffin
www.annagriffin.com

Claudia Laub
www.claudialaub.com

Jack and Lulu
www.jackandlulu.com

Kate's Paperie
www.katespaperie.com

Marcel Schurman
www.schurmanfinepapers.com

Max and Lucy
www.maxandlucy.com

Papyrus
www.papyrusonline.com

Snow and Graham
www.snowandgraham.com

Letterpress lines:

Claudia Calhoun
www.claudiacalhoun.com

Elum
www.elumdesigns.com

Julie Holcomb Printers
www.julieholcombprinters.com

Oblation Papers and Press
www.oblationpapers.com

Tryst Press
www.trystpress.com

○ INFORMATION TO INCLUDE ○

Be sure to include the following information on your invitation:

What

For Whom

When

Where

RSVP

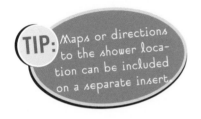

TIP: Maps or directions to the shower location can be included on a separate insert.

For example:

IT'S A GIRL!

Please join us for a baby shower
honoring

Sheryl Dickert

Thursday, April 8
7:00 p.m.

1275 - 19th Avenue
San Francisco

RSVP
Janna DeVore
(415) 221-1553

RSVP

For baby showers, a phone call is a sufficient method for RSVPing. You will want to be sure to have your guests RSVP, so you know whom to expect and especially how much food to plan on. It also helps busy guests remember the day and time of the shower once they have committed to coming. Putting the line "RSVP regrets only" is also perfectly appropriate; this assumes that everyone is coming and is a good way to handle it if you want to limit the number of phone calls.

DECORATIONS

Decorations for baby showers need not be overly involved—in fact, simple often works best. You will find that a few nicely placed touches add as much as an elaborate overhaul of a room. Decorations should follow the shower theme you have selected in style and color. Let the centerpiece for your serving table be the focal point of your decorations. By highlighting a small area, you can achieve the feeling you want for the party without going overboard. Some simple ideas are included in this chapter.

Balloons are perfect decorations for a baby shower. Bunches of balloons tied to the front porch of your home give guests a sense of celebration when they first arrive. They also make your house easier to spot for guests who are first-time visitors to your home. Balloons tied to the chair where the guest of honor will sit give the room a festive air, and the bouquet can be sent home after the shower with the mother-to-be.

A vase or bowl of flowers always makes an excellent centerpiece and can be either fun and playful or dressy and elegant depending on the flowers you chose. Always use fresh flowers! Fresh flowers highlight the fact that this is a special celebration because they last for only a few days and because, for most of us, they are something that we splurge on only every once in a while. Nothing can replace fresh flowers. Try a bunch of happy daisies or fragrant lilacs in the spring, or decorate with fresh daffodils (either potted or cut), which seem particularly suited to baby showers. In summer, add a splash of color with gerbera daisies. To keep the flower heads from drooping, wire them with thin green wire. Or you can snip off the heads and float them in a large glass

TIP: Always use fresh flowers!

TIPS ON FLOWER ARRANGING ✳

- You can buy inexpensive flowers at the grocery store, green markets, and even price clubs. Just take them home and rearrange them in a vase.

- Recut the stems so the flowers have a fresh cut to soak up water. Cut at an angle.

- Put the arrangement in an unusual container, such as a tall square vase, a flat round bowl, a tin bucket, or a ceramic pitcher.

- Include unusual greenery.

- Add cut branches, corkscrew willow, or pussy tails to give height and proportion to your arrangement.

- Use different colors of flowers to complement and contrast.

- Incorporate fresh fruit if possible. For example, fill the bottom of a clear vase with fresh blueberries, or put whole apples and oranges on bamboo skewers and include them in your arrangement.

- Tie your vase with ribbon. Ribbons can distinctly change the look of your flowers. For example, use gingham for a casual arrangement or silks for an elegant one. You can bring out the colors and style of your arrangement by the type of ribbon you select.

bowl for a stunning centerpiece. In fall, decorate using chrysanthemums, roses, or wild sunflowers. In winter, create bouquets with white lilies or use a simple orchid to make an elegant centerpiece. A fresh gardenia floating in a bowl of water is also a beautiful, fragrant choice.

Stocks, irises, snapdragons, delphiniums, and freesia are available year-round and are inexpensive flowers. Freesia is delicate and has a wonderful smell. Fresh roses are also available year-round and are often the favorite choice; they come in every color imaginable and last five days or more—a day or two longer than many fresh-cut flowers.

TIP: String up white Christmas lights for a cheerful ambiance.

Other ideas for decorations include stringing up white Christmas lights on your railing or over an outdoor canopy. They give a cheerful ambiance whether it is a wintery day with a beautiful snowfall or a lazy summer evening. You can make luminaries by putting small white votive candles in paper bags. White paper bags work well for baby showers. You can even cut out a shape in the bags, such as a star or a baby bottle. Weigh down the bags with sand to keep them from blowing or falling over. Decorate a backyard with luminaries for an outdoor shower or use them to line the walkway leading to your door.

Many decorations will be specific to your theme, whether it is sand and seashells for a beach theme or a layered cake with pink frosting and a little tiara crown on top for a princess theme. A few words of caution: don't use crepe paper—it looks cheap—and avoid making a center-piece, cake, or anything else in the shape of a baby diaper!

GAMES

There are many fun and simple games that you can play at a baby shower. Pick one or two at the most and make sure to move them along quickly. Don't get bogged down in games like crossword puzzles with baby terminology or long lists of true and false questions about baby care. Avoid games that take a long time to correct the answers. Here are a few fun games to get your guests involved in the shower. Some of them make good icebreakers as well.

⚬ DON'T SAY "BABY"! ⚬

When each guest arrives, give her two diaper pins to pin to her shirt. Explain that for the length of the shower she is not allowed to say the word "baby." If she says "baby" and someone catches her, she has to give one of her diaper pins to that person. It's fun to see how many people will forget and say the word, given the topic of your celebration. Some people even get rather aggressive in collecting diaper pins! At the end of the shower, the person who has the most pins gets a prize.

⚬ THEY EAT THAT?! ⚬

A popular game at many baby showers is to guess what type of baby food is in jars with the labels removed. Have guests see if they can guess the contents without opening the jar. If you choose foods that look similar, it can be tricky. Pick five jars of baby food. For vegetables, I'd suggest peas, green beans, carrots, sweet potatoes, and squash. For fruit, I'd try pears, peaches, bananas, plums, and blueberries. Tape a number one through five to the bottom of each jar. Make a key for yourself by writing the number and the contents of the baby food jar on a separate paper.

TIP: A popular game is to guess the types of food in baby jars.

Then remove the labels. For the game, let your guests guess which food is which. If you want the game to be easier, let them know the five foods they are choosing from. If you want it to be more difficult, don't give them any clues beyond whether you are doing fruits or veggies. Be sure, however, to get a solid baby food with just one ingredient, like pears. No fair picking apple-strawberry-pineapple mix and expecting someone to guess that!

∘ WHICH IS THE BABY STUFF? ∘

For this game you will need:
- Baby talcum powder
- Sugar
- Powdered sugar
- Flour
- Baking powder

Get five small bowls or cups. Put a little of each of the white powdery stuff into its own cup—talcum powder in one cup, sugar in another cup, and so on. Tell the guests that only one of the containers has something you would use for your baby. Pass the cups around the room. Guests are allowed to touch the powder, but not smell or taste it. See if they can figure out which is the item for baby.

○ IT'S ALL IN THE NAME ○

Go around the room and have each guest tell her favorite baby name. If you know the shower is for a girl, have guests give girl names only. If you know the shower is for a boy, then have guests give boy names. If you don't know whether the baby will be a girl or boy, then give favorite names for both. You can play the same game having guests give their *least* favorite baby names.

Least Favorite Girl Names

Bertha	*Elvira*
Mavis	*Eunice*
Fanny	*Mildred*
Princess	*Bunny*

Least Favorite Boy Names

Arvin	*Orsel*
Lester	*Horace*
Neville	*Clarence*
Clem	*Hubby*

Favorite Girl Names

Elizabeth	Abigail
Emma	Isabel
Madison	Sarah
Olivia	Morgan
Hannah	Paige

Favorite Boy Names

Jacob	Jack
Matthew	Zachary
Nate	Ryan
Andrew	James
William	Connor

∘ WHO'S THAT BABY? ∘

A couple of weeks before the shower get a baby picture from each woman who will be attending. This will take a little time, but is worth the effort. The day of the shower hang the pictures around the room (or get a large bulletin board) and give each picture a number. When guests arrive, give them paper and a pencil and let them browse the photos and try to determine which of the guests appears as a baby in which photograph. It's fun to catch a glimpse of familiarity in the photos. And this game gets guests talking to one another.

○ MEMORIZING BABY ITEMS ○

For this game, you will make a gift basket of baby items that you show around the room. Give guests sixty seconds to look at the items, and then take the basket away. Give everyone the ready signal and then time them. They have sixty seconds to write down all the items they can remember from the basket. Guests get one point per item they write down correctly. If a person writes something down that wasn't in the basket, she loses a point from her total. The person who gets the most correct items wins a prize. Then you give the gift basket to the expectant mother as your shower present. Some items you could include in your basket are listed on page 53.

LIST OF BABY ITEMS

- *Diaper pins*
- *Q-tips*
- *Bottle*
- *Bottle brush*
- *Pacifier*
- *Talcum powder*
- *Baby shampoo*
- *Baby lotion*
- *Rattle*

- *Baby washcloths*
- *Baby ear thermometer*
- *Baby wipes*
- *Burp cloths*
- *Teething ring*
- *Board book*
- *Soft toy*
- *Alphabet fridge magnets*
- *Night-light*

○ OLD WIVES' TALES ○

If your guest of honor does not know the sex of her baby, then try out these old wives' tales for determining whether she is having a boy or a girl. Even if she's had an ultrasound, you can use these crazy and very unscientific tests to check the "accuracy" of the ultrasound.

- Ask the mom-to-be if she has been having cravings for sweet food or sour food. Sweet cravings mean she's having a girl. Sour cravings mean she's having a boy.

- If the mom-to-be is carrying the baby low, it's a boy. If she is carrying the baby high, it's a girl.
- If the mother's age at conception and the year of conception are both even or both odd, the baby is a girl. If one is even and one is odd, the baby is a boy.
- Ask the mom if she's been unusually crabby during this pregnancy. If so, it means she's having a girl.
- Tie a ring onto a string or hold a necklace over the mother-to-be's belly. If it moves from side to side, she's having a boy. If it moves in a circular motion, she's having a girl.
- If the mom was the more aggressive partner when the baby was conceived, the baby will be a boy. If the father was the more aggressive, the baby will be a girl.
- Ask the mother-to-be to show her hands. If she shows them palms up, it's a girl; palms down, it's a boy.
- Finally, just ask the mom what she thinks she's having. In a study that asked women with no previous knowledge about their baby's sex, the moms-to-be correctly guessed the sex of their baby over 70 percent of the time.

◦ MORE CASUAL FUN ◦

For a shower with fewer people, close friends, or older guests, it can be relaxing just to sit and talk while you put together a puzzle with a baby theme. An Anne Geddes puzzle is especially fun. Another laid-back way to spend your shower time is to tie a baby quilt. Buy the fabric and batting beforehand and have the quilt set up with chairs around it. Then guests can tie the quilt during the shower and give it as a group gift to the mother-to-be.

RECIPES

Showers lend themselves well to finger foods and dainty appetizers, salads, light lunches, Sunday brunches, or just lovely desserts. The following recipes were chosen for their taste, presentation, ease of preparation, and general appeal. You can use these recipes separately, combine them into menus, or add your own favorite recipes to create the perfect menu for your baby shower.

◦ CHOOSING INGREDIENTS ◦

When shopping for fresh produce and baked goods, it is best to buy them the day of the shower or the day before, if possible, to ensure the most freshness. Farmers markets and green grocers are often the best places to get ripe, organic, beautiful fruits and vegetables. Even if you don't shop there regularly, consider doing so when cooking for a party. Also keep in mind with the following recipes, as with any, that you do not have to be a stickler for every specific ingredient. If your salad calls for pomegranate seeds and pomegranates are out of season, substitute craisins or fresh strawberry slices. If your recipe calls for bell peppers, but the bell peppers look withered, see if your recipe will still work if you leave them out altogether. Pay attention to the ingredients and never force a menu if the ingredients won't live up to it. Otherwise the food will suffer.

TIP: Consider farmers markets and green grocers for ripe, beautiful produce.

◦ PRESENTATION ◦

Presentation can be nine-tenths of the success of a dish. The value of a beautiful garnish can't be overstated. A glass of pineapple-orange punch is fine, but a glass of pineapple-orange punch garnished with lemon and orange

GARNISHES

Here are some simple garnishes to keep in mind. Their addition to the right dish can change it from something good to something fabulous.

- *Fresh herbs*
- *Shaved chocolate*
- *Whole or chopped nuts*
- *Fresh berries or slices of fresh fruit*
- *Drizzled syrups*
- *Coconut*
- *Small candies or sprinkles*

slices and a maraschino cherry is something special. A simple slice of chocolate cake can be dressed up by drizzling raspberry syrup in a zigzag pattern over a white plate, and adding a few fresh raspberries and a sprig of mint on the side. That's the difference between a piece of cake that's not long remembered and a dessert at your favorite restaurant for which you pay five dollars. It's really the same piece of cake—it's all in the presentation.

☀ APPETIZERS ☀

Combine these appetizers to make a lovely buffet or serve them along with the lunch recipes later in this chapter.

TOMATOES AND MOZZARELLA

4 large ripe tomatoes (or 6 ripe Roma tomatoes), cut into ¼-inch
    slices
2 pounds fresh mozzarella cheese, cut into ¼-inch slices
¼ to ½ cup chopped fresh basil
olive oil
freshly ground sea salt
freshly ground black pepper

Arrange tomato slices and mozzarella slices alternately on a serving platter. Sprinkle with basil. Drizzle with olive oil. Sprinkle with salt and pepper to taste. Garnish with a bigger sprig of basil.

Makes 8 to 12 servings

CUCUMBER SANDWICHES

1 3-ounce package cream
   cheese, softened
½ teaspoon garlic salt
1 teaspoon chopped chives
8 slices white bread

½ seedless cucumber, thinly
   sliced
chives for garnish, cut in 2-inch
   lengths

Combine cream cheese, garlic salt, and chives in a
bowl. Mix well. Cover and chill for 1 hour.

Spread each piece of bread with cream cheese mixture.
Using a serrated bread knife, carefully slice off crusts,
cutting off as little of the white part of the bread as
possible. Cut each piece of bread into 4 square pieces,
or 3 longer pieces. Alternately you can use cookie cutters to cut the bread into different shapes.

Make a tiny stacked sandwich with a layer of bread,
then a layer of cucumber, then a layer of bread, until
you have 3 layers of bread and 2 layers of cucumber.
Cover with plastic wrap and refrigerate until ready to
serve. Garnish with chives.

Makes 8 to 10 servings

BLACK BEAN AND MANGO SALSA

1 15-ounce can black beans, drained
3 cups chopped mango
1 cup chopped red onion
2 tablespoons chopped cilantro
2 tablespoons olive oil
2 teaspoons cumin
2 teaspoons lime juice
salt and pepper to taste

Combine beans, mango, onion, and cilantro in a mixing bowl. Add oil, cumin, lime juice, and salt and pepper; mix well. Serve immediately or chill until just before serving.

Makes 12 servings

Serve with tortilla chips.

Blue Cheese, Bacon, and Garlic Dip

7 slices bacon, chopped
2 cloves garlic, minced
8 ounces cream cheese, softened
¼ cup half-and-half
1 cup crumbled blue cheese

2 tablespoons chopped fresh
 chives
3 tablespoons chopped smoked
 almonds

Cook bacon in a large skillet over medium-high heat until almost crisp, about 7 minutes. Drain excess fat from skillet. Add garlic and cook until bacon is crisp, about 3 minutes.

Preheat oven to 350 degrees. In a medium-sized bowl, beat cream cheese until smooth. Add half-and-half and mix until combined. Stir in bacon mixture, blue cheese, and chives. Transfer to a small ovenproof serving dish and cover with foil. Bake until thoroughly heated, or about 30 minutes. Sprinkle with chopped almonds.

Makes 2 cups

Serve with sliced apples, sliced pears, crackers, or french bread.

Stuffed Mushrooms

½ cup grated swiss cheese
¼ cup fine dry bread crumbs, plain
1 small garlic clove, finely minced
2 tablespoons butter, at room temperature
24 large mushrooms
¼ cup butter, melted

In a bowl, combine cheese, bread crumbs, garlic, and 2 tablespoons butter. Blend well. Wash mushrooms and remove stems. Place unfilled mushrooms on a baking sheet, rounded side up. Brush with melted butter and broil for 2 to 3 minutes, about 4 inches from heat.

Remove baking sheet from broiler; turn mushrooms over. Fill mushrooms with cheese mixture. Return filled mushrooms to the oven and broil for 1 to 2 minutes longer. Serve immediately.

Makes 8 servings

CHILLED ASPARAGUS

2 pounds fresh asparagus, trimmed
lettuce leaves for serving

For Dressing:

¼ cup white wine vinegar

2 teaspoons Dijon mustard

3 tablespoons minced
    crystallized ginger

¼ teaspoon salt

½ teaspoon freshly ground pepper

½ cup vegetable oil

Blanch asparagus by placing in boiling water for 1 to 2 minutes. Remove from boiling water and plunge into ice water. Drain and chill.

To make ginger dressing, blend vinegar, mustard, ginger, salt, and pepper in a food processor. With the machine running, slowly add the oil in a thin stream. When ready to serve, arrange chilled asparagus on a bed of lettuce leaves and drizzle with ginger dressing.

Makes 6 to 8 servings

BAKED BRIE

1 package frozen puff pastry sheets
1 egg
1 tablespoon water
1 15-ounce wheel brie

Preheat oven to 350 degrees. Thaw pastry sheets at room temperature. Make an egg wash by combining egg and water. Open and flatten pastry sheets. Place whole wheel of brie in the center and wrap pastry sheets to cover brie. Cut off excess pastry dough and form the loose ends of the dough together to make a seam. Seal seam with egg wash. Place seam side down on a baking sheet. Brush top and sides with egg wash and bake 20 minutes or until pastry is golden brown. Let stand for 1 hour before serving.

Makes 8 servings

Serve with clusters of red grapes.

NOTE: *You can cut out shapes, such as leaves or flowers, from the excess dough and place on top of the wrapped brie before baking. You can also cut the pastry dough into strips and make a woven pattern over the brie instead of wrapping it completely.*

✳ BRUNCHES ✳

These recipes are perfect for a Saturday or Sunday brunch. Serve a variety of rolls and breads with different fruit recipes, or make a buffet brunch with several of these options.

ZUCCHINI BREAD

3 cups flour, sifted

1 tablespoon cinnamon

1 teaspoon salt

1 teaspoon baking soda

¼ teaspoon baking powder

3 eggs, beaten

1 cup sugar

1 cup firmly packed brown sugar

1 cup vegetable oil

1 tablespoon vanilla

2 cups grated zucchini

½ cup chopped nuts (optional)

Preheat oven to 325 degrees. Sift flour, cinnamon, salt, baking soda, and baking powder together. Set aside. In a large bowl, thoroughly beat eggs, sugar, brown sugar, oil, and vanilla. Stir sifted ingredients into egg mixture. Blend in zucchini and nuts if using. Pour into two greased and lightly floured 4½ x 8½-inch loaf tins. Bake for 60 to 70 minutes.

Makes 16 servings

Easy Cinnamon Rolls

For Rolls:

1 loaf frozen bread dough, thawed	½ cup chopped pecans
2 tablespoons butter, melted	1 teaspoon cinnamon
⅔ cup brown sugar	⅓ cup heavy cream

For Icing:

⅔ cup powdered sugar	dash vanilla
1 tablespoon milk	

Roll dough into a rectangle shape, about 18 x 6 inches. Brush with melted butter. In a bowl, combine brown sugar, pecans, and cinnamon; sprinkle over dough. Starting at long edge, roll up dough, jelly-roll fashion. Moisten edges and seal. Cut roll into 20 slices using thread. Place rolls, cut side down, into 2 lightly buttered round cake pans. Let rise for about 1½ hours, or until doubled. Pour the cream over the rolls, and then bake at 350 degrees for 25 minutes.

To make icing, combine powdered sugar, milk, and vanilla, adding more sugar or milk to reach desired consistency. Drizzle over rolls while still warm.

Makes 20 cinnamon rolls

ORANGE FRENCH TOAST

4 eggs	pinch salt
⅔ cup orange juice	8 slices day-old regular white
½ cup milk	bread or french bread sliced
1 tablespoon sugar	½ inch thick
1 teaspoon vanilla	powdered sugar for dusting
¼ teaspoon cinnamon	butter and maple syrup for
1 teaspoon grated orange rind	serving

Lightly beat eggs in a bowl. Add orange juice, milk, sugar, vanilla, cinnamon, orange rind, and salt. Mix well. Dip bread slices in egg mixture, turning to coat both sides. Brown both sides on a hot, preheated griddle that has been buttered or sprayed with nonstick cooking spray. Repeat until all slices of bread have been browned. Lightly dust with powdered sugar and serve with butter and warm maple syrup.

Makes 4 servings

NOTE: *Put cooked french toast on a plate in a warm oven to keep it hot while you cook the remaining slices.*

Blueberry Scones

For Scones:

2 cups flour

2 tablespoons sugar

2 teaspoons baking powder

½ teaspoon baking soda

½ teaspoon salt

¼ cup butter, cut in pieces

1 cup blueberries

1 tablespoon flour

⅔ cup buttermilk

1 egg

For Topping:

1 teaspoon buttermilk

1 to 2 tablespoons sugar

Preheat oven to 425 degrees. Grease baking sheet.
Combine flour, sugar, baking powder, baking soda, and
salt in a large bowl. With pastry blender or two knives,
cut in butter until mixture resembles coarse meal. Toss
blueberries with 1 tablespoon flour and then stir into

the flour mixture. In a separate bowl, beat buttermilk and egg. Pour into dry ingredients and stir with fork until mixture comes together.

On a lightly floured surface, knead dough 5 or 6 times. Transfer to prepared baking sheet. With floured hands, pat into an 8-inch square. Cut into nine 2½-inch squares. (Do not separate.) Just before baking, brush with 1 teaspoon buttermilk and sprinkle with 1 to 2 tablespoons sugar. Bake 14 to 16 minutes, until golden. Transfer to wire rack. Serve warm.

Makes 9 scones

CHEESE BLINTZES

For Batter:

2 eggs

2 tablespoons oil

1 cup milk

¾ cup sifted flour

½ teaspoon salt

For Filling:

4 ounces cream cheese

2 egg yolks

4 ounces cottage cheese

2 tablespoons sugar

1 teaspoon vanilla

For Garnish:

sour cream, fresh berries, jam, and/or marmalade

Beat eggs, oil, and milk together in a medium-sized bowl. Add flour and salt, beating until very smooth. Chill batter for 30 minutes; it should be the consistency of heavy cream. (If it is too thick, add a little more milk.)

Grease a hot 8-inch skillet with a light coating of butter. Pour ⅛ to ¼ cup batter into the skillet, turning pan to coat it. Fry lightly on one side. Repeat with remaining batter. Stack crepes, separated with wax paper, browned side up.

To make filling, beat cream cheese, egg yolks, cottage cheese, sugar, and vanilla together until smooth. Fill each crepe with 2 heaping tablespoons of filling. Fold in ends over filling, and then roll up. Heat 2 tablespoons butter in a large skillet and fry the blintzes until browned on all sides. Garnish with sour cream, berries, jam, or marmalade as desired.

Makes 10 to 12 blintzes

DOUBLE CHOCOLATE MUFFINS

1 devil's food cake mix
1 small box instant chocolate
    pudding mix
¾ cup water
3 eggs, beaten

¼ cup sour cream
¼ cup vegetable oil
¼ teaspoon almond extract
¾ cup chocolate chips

Preheat oven to 350 degrees. Grease and flour muffin pan or use paper liners. Mix together cake mix, pudding mix, water, eggs, sour cream, oil, and almond extract on low speed until smooth. Stir in chocolate chips. Fill muffin cups three-fourths full; do not overfill. Bake 25 to 30 minutes, or until toothpick inserted in center comes out clean.

Makes 12 muffins

QUICHE LORRAINE

1 refrigerated piecrust, at room temperature*
4 to 6 slices bacon, cooked until crisp and crumbled
1 cup grated swiss cheese
⅓ cup finely chopped green onion
4 eggs
2 cups heavy whipping cream
¼ teaspoon salt
¼ teaspoon pepper

Preheat oven to 425 degrees. Line a glass pie pan or quiche dish with piecrust and crimp edges. Sprinkle bacon, cheese, and onion in pastry-lined dish.

In a large bowl, beat eggs slightly, and then beat in cream, salt, and pepper. Pour into quiche dish. Bake 15 minutes, and then reduce oven temperature to 300 degrees. Bake about 30 minutes longer or until knife inserted in center comes out clean. Let stand 10 minutes before cutting.

Makes 8 servings

*If you have a favorite piecrust recipe, you can substitute it.

STRAWBERRY-YOGURT PARFAIT

12 strawberries, sliced and divided in 4 parts
4 6-ounce containers strawberry yogurt
1 cup granola, divided in 4 parts
4 parfait glasses

In a parfait glass, layer half of one part strawberries, then half container of yogurt, and then half one part granola. Repeat with remaining one part strawberries, remaining container of yogurt, and remaining one part granola.

Repeat this process for the 3 remaining parfait glasses. Serve immediately.

Makes 4 servings

FRESH FRUIT SALAD

For Dressing:

¼ cup orange juice

2 tablespoons honey

For Salad:

2 green apples, unpeeled and sliced

2 cups fresh pineapple chunks

2 cups fresh hulled strawberries

1 cup fresh blueberries

In a small bowl, whisk together orange juice and honey to make dressing; set aside. In a large bowl, combine apples, pineapple, strawberries, and blueberries. Pour dressing over top and toss gently to coat. Refrigerate at least one half hour before serving.

Makes 8 servings

Melon Kebobs

1 cup honeydew melon chunks
1 cup cantaloupe chunks
1 cup watermelon chunks
1 cup fresh strawberries
6 metal or bamboo skewers

Combine fruit on skewers, alternating colors to make a pleasing presentation.

Makes 6 servings

✳ LUNCHES ✳

The following recipes make excellent lunches for baby showers. They can also be combined with different appetizers and desserts to make an evening dinner.

SPINACH POMEGRANATE SALAD

1 package baby spinach
seeds of ½ pomegranate
4 tablespoons crumbled blue
   cheese

3 green onions, trimmed and
   sliced
Italian salad dressing

Wash spinach and pat dry with paper towels. Put in a large bowl. Add pomegranate seeds, blue cheese, and onions. Toss with your favorite Italian salad dressing and serve.

Makes 8 servings

CHICKEN AND WILD RICE SALAD

For Salad:

1 cup wild rice, uncooked

3 14-ounce cans chicken broth

3 tablespoons lemon juice

4 boneless, skinless chicken
breasts, cooked and cut into
bite-sized pieces

3 green onions, sliced, including
dark green tops

½ red bell pepper, diced

2 ounces sugar snap peas, cut
in 1-inch pieces

1 cup pecan halves, toasted
(optional)

2 avocados, cut in chunks

For Dressing:

2 garlic cloves, minced

1 tablespoon Dijon mustard

½ teaspoon salt

¼ teaspoon pepper

¼ teaspoon sugar

¼ cup red wine vinegar

⅓ cup vegetable oil

Rinse rice and cook in the chicken broth 45 minutes to
1 hour. Drain excess broth and toss rice with lemon

juice. Cool. Add chicken, green onions, red bell pepper, and peas.

If using, toast the pecans on a baking sheet in oven at 350 degrees for about 5 minutes. Check frequently to make sure they don't burn.

Mix all the dressing ingredients together and pour over the rice salad. Just before serving, add the avocados and pecans.

Makes 6 to 8 servings

Antipasto Pasta Salad

1 16-ounce package spiral pasta
1 cup broccoli florets, blanched
3 cups cherry tomatoes, halved
½ pound provolone cheese, julienned
¼ pound salami, julienned
¼ pound sliced pepperoni, cut in half

1 large red, yellow, or green bell pepper, julienned
1 can black olives, drained
1 4-ounce jar pimientos, drained
1 8-ounce bottle Italian salad dressing or more

Bring a large pot of lightly salted water to a boil. Add pasta and cook for 8 to 10 minutes or until al dente. Drain and rinse with cold water. Blanch broccoli by placing in boiling water for 1 to 2 minutes. Remove from boiling water and plunge into ice water. Drain.

In a large bowl, combine pasta with broccoli, tomatoes, cheese, salami, pepperoni, pepper, olives, and pimientos. Pour dressing over pasta mixture and toss to coat.

Makes 8 servings

Serve with baguette.

WILTED SPINACH SALAD

For Dressing:

2 tablespoons sesame seeds

½ cup vegetable or peanut oil

¼ cup soy sauce

2 tablespoons lemon juice

2 tablespoons grated onion

½ teaspoon sugar

¼ teaspoon pepper or to taste

For Salad:

1 package baby spinach

1 large avocado, cut in strips

1 can water chestnuts, drained
   and sliced

Preheat oven to 350 degrees. Put sesame seeds onto a pie plate and bake until golden brown; cool. In a small bowl, combine sesame seeds, oil, soy sauce, lemon juice, onion, sugar, and pepper.

Wash spinach and pat dry with paper towels. Place in a serving bowl and add avocado and water chestnuts; gently toss to combine. Pour dressing over salad and refrigerate for 1 hour before serving.

Makes 8 servings

Serve with Baked Brie (see recipe on page 66) and fresh strawberries or red grapes.

Layered Southwest Salad

1 package spring mix salad greens
2 Roma tomatoes, seeded and diced
1 cucumber, peeled and diced
1 small can whole kernel corn, drained
1 red bell pepper, diced
1 cup julienned jicama
1 15-ounce can black beans, rinsed and drained
1 cup grated Mexican blend cheese
4 green onions, sliced
4 chicken breasts grilled and diced (optional)
spicy ranch salad dressing
tortilla chips (optional)

Wash lettuce and pat dry with paper towels. In a large glass bowl, layer lettuce, then tomatoes, cucumber, corn, red bell pepper, jicama, black beans, cheese, green onions, and chicken if using. Serve with spicy ranch salad dressing and tortilla chips if desired.

Makes 8 servings

ROMAINE AND GREEN APPLE SALAD

1 package hearts of romaine
2 green apples
balsamic vinaigrette

Wash lettuce and pat dry with paper towels. Break into
bite-sized pieces into a large bowl. Leaving skins on,
core green apples and chop into bite-sized pieces. Add
apples to lettuce and toss with balsamic vinaigrette.

Makes 12 servings

BAKED POTATO SOUP

4 cups chicken broth

6 medium potatoes, peeled and
  cubed

1 rib celery, minced

½ white onion, minced

3 cups half-and-half

1 cup grated sharp cheddar
  cheese

2 teaspoons salt

1 teaspoon pepper

6 strips bacon, cooked and
  crumbled, for garnish

4 green onions, trimmed and
  sliced, for garnish

Bring chicken broth, potatoes, celery, and onion to a boil
in a stockpot. Cover and simmer over medium-low heat
for 20 minutes, stirring occasionally. Turn heat to low
and add half-and-half, cheese, salt, and pepper. Simmer,
uncovered, 5 to 8 minutes, stirring constantly. Pour into
bowls and garnish with bacon and green onions.

Makes 6 servings

Serve with a green salad or corn bread.

Zesty Minestrone Soup

4 medium garlic cloves, minced

½ cup diced onion

1½ cups sliced carrots

1 cup chopped celery

2 cups finely shredded cabbage

1 cup diced zucchini

3 tablespoons olive oil

8 cups water

1 28-ounce can crushed tomatoes

2 15-ounce cans kidney beans

¼ cup pearl barley (optional)

1½ teaspoons salt or to taste

1 teaspoon pepper or to taste

2 bay leaves

2 teaspoons oregano

2 teaspoons basil

¼ teaspoon chili powder

garlic croutons for garnish
   (optional)

Sauté garlic, onion, carrots, celery, cabbage, and zucchini in olive oil until vegetables are soft. Put vegetables in a large stockpot and add water, tomatoes, kidney beans, and barley if using. Stir in salt, pepper, bay leaves, oregano, basil, and chili powder. Simmer 30 minutes to 1 hour or until heated through. Adjust seasonings to taste. Garnish with garlic croutons, if desired.

Makes 10 to 12 servings

Serve with hard rolls.

CHICKEN-SALAD CROISSANTS

6 double chicken breasts   2 cups red seedless grapes
1 cup cashews   12 croissants

For Dressing:
2 cups mayonnaise   1 celery stalk, diced
juice of 2 lemons   1 bunch green onions, sliced

Preheat oven to 350 degrees. Salt chicken breasts, cover with foil, and bake in a glass dish for 40 minutes. Be careful not to overbake or chicken will be too dry. When cooked, put chicken in fridge to cool; when it is cool enough to handle, cut into small cubes.

In a medium bowl, make dressing by combining mayonnaise, lemon juice, celery, and onions. Add more lemon juice if dressing is too thick. Pour dressing over chicken and mix well. Chill for 3 to 4 hours to let flavors blend. Right before serving, fold in nuts and grapes. Serve on sliced croissants.

Makes 12 servings

Serve with Fresh Fruit Salad (see recipe on page 77).

CRISPY COCONUT SHRIMP

12 jumbo shrimp, peeled and deveined
½ teaspoon garlic and herb seasoning
¼ teaspoon pepper
¾ cup flour
1 egg, well beaten
¼ cup coconut

Preheat oven to 425 degrees. Spray a large baking
sheet with nonstick cooking spray. Sprinkle shrimp
evenly with seasoning blend and pepper. Place flour,
egg, and coconut in 3 separate bowls. Dip shrimp first
in egg, then flour, then back in egg, and then roll
generously in coconut. Arrange shrimp on baking sheet.
Bake 12 to 15 minutes or until golden and crisp.

Makes 4 servings

Serve with white or brown rice.

Artichoke Pizza

1 refrigerated pizza crust
2 tablespoons pesto
8 ounces provolone cheese
½ cup grated Parmesan cheese
4 Roma tomatoes, sliced

1 can artichoke hearts, drained
  and chopped
¼ cup fresh basil leaves, torn
freshly ground pepper to taste

For Pesto:
1 cup extra-virgin olive oil
1 large garlic clove, minced
10 to 12 fresh basil leaves, minced
½ to 1 bunch parsley, minced

Preheat oven to 350 degrees. Fit pizza crust on a
9 x 13-inch baking sheet and bake according to package
directions. Make pesto by combining oil, garlic, basil,
and parsley. Brush crust with pesto, then layer provolone
and Parmesan cheese, tomatoes, and artichoke hearts.
Sprinkle with fresh basil and pepper. Bake for 10 minutes
or until cheese is melted and bubbly.

Makes 12 servings

✳ DESSERTS ✳

From rich chocolate cakes to sweetly decorated cookies, and tangy fruit cobblers to light and fluffy combinations, nothing makes the perfect baby shower as easily as the perfect dessert.

FIVE LAYER BARS

1 cup graham cracker crumbs
½ cup margarine, melted
1 cup semisweet chocolate chips

1 cup coconut
1 cup chopped pecans or walnuts
1 can sweetened condensed milk

Stir graham cracker crumbs into melted margarine. Pat crumb mixture evenly into the bottom of an ungreased 9 x 13-inch pan. Sprinkle chocolate chips, then coconut, and then nuts evenly over top. Drizzle with sweetened condensed milk.

Bake at 350 degrees for 30 minutes. Cool for 1 hour and cut into bars.

Makes 12 large or 24 small bars

CHOCOLATE CREAM CAKE

1 package devil's food cake mix
1 8-ounce container frozen whipped topping, thawed
6 tablespoons butter, softened
½ cup cocoa powder
2⅔ cups powdered sugar
⅓ cup milk
1 teaspoon vanilla extract
8 ounces chocolate shavings (optional)
fresh raspberries (optional)

Grease and flour two 8-inch round cake pans. Make cake according to package directions. When cake is completely cool, place one layer on a serving dish. Top with whipped topping, spreading evenly, leaving about ½-inch border around the edge of the cake with no topping. Gently place the second layer of cake on top and press down very lightly to set the layers.

In a medium bowl, cream the butter with an electric mixer. Add cocoa and powdered sugar alternately with milk. Beat to desired spreading consistency, adding more milk if needed. Blend in vanilla. Frost top and sides of cake with frosting.

Sprinkle top and sides of cake with chocolate shavings if using and garnish each cut slice of cake with fresh raspberries if desired.

Makes 10 servings

Sunshine Cheesecake

For Crust:

1½ 8-ounce bags ginger snap cookies, ground

6 tablespoons butter, melted

1½ teaspoons minced orange zest

For Filling:

1½ cups fresh orange juice

1 3-inch piece of unpeeled fresh ginger, thinly sliced

4 8-ounce packages cream cheese, at room temperature

⅔ cup sugar

1 tablespoon minced orange zest

1 tablespoon vanilla

8 ounces Lindt white chocolate, melted

4 eggs

fresh mint leaves for garnish

Stir all ingredients for crust in a medium-sized bowl until crumbs are moist. Press into bottom and 2 inches up sides of a springform pan.

To make filling, preheat oven to 350 degrees. Boil orange juice with ginger in a heavy saucepan until it is reduced to about 3 tablespoons of liquid. This will take about 12 minutes. Using an electric mixer, beat the cream cheese, sugar, orange zest, and vanilla in a large bowl until smooth. Strain reduced orange juice and add to cream cheese mixture. With the mixer running, add the melted chocolate and beat until combined. With mixer on low speed add eggs, one at a time, beating until combined.

Pour the batter into the crust and bake until top is dry and sides puff slightly, about 50 minutes. (Cheesecake will still jiggle when shaken.) Transfer to wire rack and cool. Cover and chill overnight before serving. Garnish each slice of cheesecake with fresh mint leaves.

Makes 12 servings

Sugar Cookies

For Cookies:

½ cup butter, softened

½ cup sugar

2 eggs

1 teaspoon vanilla

2½ cups flour, sifted

2 teaspoons baking powder

For Icing:

1 cup powdered sugar

2 teaspoons milk

2 teaspoons light corn syrup

¼ teaspoon almond extract

assorted food coloring

Cream together butter and sugar. Beat in eggs and vanilla. Add dry ingredients, a little at a time, until incorporated. Chill dough for 2 to 4 hours before rolling out.

Preheat oven to 375 degrees. Roll out dough on a lightly floured surface to ¼ inch thick. Cut into desired shapes with cookie cutters. Bake 7 to 12 minutes. Cool, ice, and decorate as desired.

To make icing, stir together powdered sugar and milk in a small bowl until smooth. Beat in corn syrup and almond extract until icing is smooth and glossy. If icing is too thick, add more corn syrup. Divide icing into separate bowls and add food coloring to each to achieve desired intensity. You can dip your sugar cookies, paint them with a brush, or spread the icing using a butter knife.

Makes 2 dozen cookies

FLAN

1¼ cups sugar	1 condensed milk can full of
6 eggs	water
1 can sweetened condensed milk	1 teaspoon vanilla

Preheat oven to 350 degrees. Caramelize sugar in a skillet over medium-high heat, being careful not to burn. Pour the caramelized sugar into a loaf pan. In a bowl, blend eggs, then add condensed milk and blend more. Add water and vanilla and blend well. Pour egg mixture over caramel mixture in loaf pan. Fill a 9 x 13-inch cake pan about 1½ inches with water. Set loaf pan in pan with water and bake in oven for 45 minutes.

Makes 8 servings

PUMPKIN CHOCOLATE CHIP CAKE

4 eggs
1 cup oil
2 cups sugar
1 29-ounce can pumpkin
3 cups flour
1 teaspoon salt

2 teaspoons cinnamon
2 teaspoons baking soda
2 teaspoons baking powder
1 8-ounce bag semisweet
    chocolate chips
flour for dusting

Preheat oven to 350 degrees. Grease and flour a Bundt cake pan. In a large bowl, mix together eggs, oil, sugar, and pumpkin. In a separate bowl, mix together flour, salt, cinnamon, baking soda, and baking powder. Add the flour mixture to the pumpkin mixture and mix well.

In a small bowl, lightly coat chocolate chips with flour. Add three-fourths of the chocolate chips to the pumpkin batter. Pour batter into pan and sprinkle the rest of the chocolate chips on top. Bake 1 hour. Cool for 10 to 15 minutes, and then invert on a serving plate.

Makes 16 servings

PINEAPPLE NUT CAKE

For Cake:

½ cup butter, softened

2 cups sugar

2 eggs

2 teaspoons vanilla

1 20-ounce can crushed
  pineapple with juice

2 cups flour

2 teaspoons baking soda

½ cup chopped pecans

For Frosting:

1 8-ounce package cream
  cheese, softened

½ cup butter, softened

1⅓ cups powdered sugar

1 teaspoon vanilla

½ cup chopped pecans

To make cake, preheat oven to 350 degrees. In a large mixing bowl, cream butter with sugar. Add eggs, vanilla, and pineapple. Add flour and baking soda; mix well. Fold in nuts. Pour into a greased 9 x 13-inch pan and bake 35 to 40 minutes.

To make frosting, combine cream cheese, butter, powdered sugar, and vanilla in a medium-sized mixing bowl; mix until blended. Spread over cooled cake. Sprinkle with nuts.

Makes 12 servings

Peach and Blueberry Cobbler

For Filling:

1½ tablespoons cornstarch

¼ teaspoon ground mace

½ cup firmly packed brown
sugar

¼ cup water

1 tablespoon lemon juice

1 tablespoon butter

5 cups sliced peaches

1 cup fresh or frozen blueberries

For Topping:

1 cup flour

1½ teaspoons baking powder

2 tablespoons sugar

⅛ teaspoon salt

4 tablespoons butter, softened

1 egg, slightly beaten

¼ cup milk

To make filling, combine cornstarch, mace, brown
sugar, and water in a medium-sized saucepan and cook
over medium heat, stirring until thickened. Remove
from heat. Add lemon juice and butter, and then fold
in fruit.

To make topping, sift together flour, baking powder,
sugar, and salt in a small mixing bowl. Cut in butter

until mixture is like coarse meal. In a separate bowl, combine egg and milk; add to dry ingredients. Stir just until moistened.

Preheat oven to 400 degrees. Pour fruit filling into a large 1½ to 2-quart baking dish. Spoon topping over filling. Bake 20 to 25 minutes.

Makes 6 to 8 servings

Serve warm with whipped cream or vanilla ice cream.

Strawberry Rhubarb Pie

For Crumb Topping:

1 cup flour

½ cup sugar

¼ cup butter, softened

For Pie:

1 9-inch piecrust

2 cups 1-inch-thick rhubarb slices

2 cups strawberries, halved if needed

1 cup sugar (or more if desired)

4 tablespoons flour

½ teaspoon lemon juice

1 teaspoon salt

To make topping, combine flour, sugar, and butter. Mix with your hands until large crumbs form. Set aside.

Preheat oven to 425 degrees. Press piecrust into pie plate and crimp edges. Combine the rhubarb, strawberries, sugar, flour, lemon juice, and salt. Pour into unbaked piecrust and bake 30 minutes. Remove from oven and sprinkle crumb mixture on top. Bake

15 minutes more or until crumbs are brown and pie is bubbly. Cool on rack.

Makes 8 servings

Serve with vanilla ice cream.

NOTE: *Rhubarb is tart. Depending on your taste, you might want to add more sugar.*

POPPY SEED CAKE

For Cake:

1 package Duncan Hines yellow
cake mix

1 small box vanilla instant
pudding

4 eggs

½ cup oil

1¼ cups hot water

2 teaspoons almond extract

2 tablespoons poppy seeds

For Glaze:

1 cup powdered sugar

3 to 4 teaspoons lemon juice

To make cake, preheat oven to 350 degrees. Grease and flour a Bundt cake pan. Beat cake mix, pudding mix, eggs, oil, and hot water for 3 minutes with an electric mixer. Add almond extract and poppy seeds. Bake according to cake mix package directions or until a tooth-pick inserted into the cake comes out clean. Cool for 10 to 15 minutes before inverting pan on serving plate.

To make glaze, blend together powdered sugar and lemon juice to desired consistency. Drizzle over cake.

Makes 16 servings

LEMONADE PIE

For Crust:

4 cups boxed Oreo cookie
crumbs or plain graham
cracker crumbs

1 cup sugar
1 cup butter, melted

For Filling:

½ gallon vanilla ice cream

1 12-ounce can pink lemonade frozen concentrate

Preheat oven to 350 degrees. To make crust, mix together cookie or cracker crumbs, sugar, and butter; stir until crumbs are moist. Press into 2 pie tins. Bake the crusts for 7 minutes. Allow to cool before adding the filling.

To make filling, soften the ice cream and thaw the lemonade. In a large bowl, fold the undiluted lemonade into the ice cream until smooth. Pour into crusts, freeze until solid, and then serve.

Makes 16 servings

Key Lime Pie

For Crust:

2 cups graham cracker crumbs   ½ cup butter, melted
½ cup sugar

For Filling:

1 can sweetened condensed milk   ½ cup key lime juice
3 egg yolks

For Topping:

1 pint whipping cream, sweetened

To make crust, in a medium-sized bowl, mix graham cracker crumbs, sugar, and butter together. Press evenly into the bottom and sides of a pie pan.

To make filling, beat together sweetened condensed milk, egg yolks, and key lime juice until smooth. Pour into piecrust and bake at 350 degrees for 15 minutes. Allow to stand 10 minutes before refrigerating. Refrigerate until cool.

Top with whipped cream before serving.

Makes 12 servings

LEMON BARS

For Crust:

1¼ cups butter or margarine   ½ cup powdered sugar
2¼ cups flour

For Filling:

4 eggs   4 tablespoons flour
2 cups sugar   1 teaspoon baking powder
6 tablespoons lemon juice   powdered sugar for dusting

To make crust, preheat oven to 350 degrees. In a
bowl, beat butter or margarine with an electric mixer
until softened. Add flour and powdered sugar and mix
on low until just combined. Spread dough evenly in a
9 x 13-inch baking pan. Bake 10 minutes and then
remove from oven.

To make filling, in a small mixing bowl, mix together eggs,
sugar, lemon juice, flour, and baking powder on low for just
a few minutes. Do not overmix. Pour on top of partially
baked crust. Return to oven and bake 30 to 35 minutes.
Allow to cool slightly and then dust with powdered sugar.
Cut into bars.

Makes 18 large or 24 small bars

Mixed-Berry Stacks

1 package frozen puff pastry, thawed
4½ tablespoons unsalted butter, melted
2 cups strawberries, sliced
1 cup blueberries
1 cup blackberries
6 tablespoons sugar
3 tablespoons lemon juice
whipping cream, sweetened

Preheat oven to 350 degrees. Place 1 thawed puff pastry sheet on a dry and floured countertop. Cut out pastry in circles using a drinking glass or cookie cutter. Place circles on a baking sheet sprayed with nonstick cooking spray and prick with a fork. Repeat with second sheet of puff pastry. Repeat until you have used all the sheets. Bake pastry rounds 10 to 15 minutes, or until golden. When the pastries are baked, remove them from the pan and place on a cooling rack.

While pastry rounds are baking, toss together berries, sugar, and lemon juice in a bowl until well combined.

To assemble, arrange 1 pastry round on a plate and top
with ¼ cup berry mixture. Add a second round and
top with ¼ cup berry mixture. Top with a third round.
Repeat this until you have made 8 berry stacks with
3 layers. Top each with a dollop of whipped cream.

Makes 8 servings

Snickerdoodles

1 cup butter

1½ cups sugar

2 eggs

2¾ cups flour

2 teaspoons cream of tartar

2 teaspoons baking soda

¼ teaspoon salt

2 tablespoons sugar

2 tablespoons cinnamon

In a large bowl, cream butter, sugar, and eggs with an electric mixer on medium speed until light and fluffy. Scrape sides of bowl occasionally. In a separate bowl, combine flour, cream of tartar, baking soda, and salt. Add to creamed mixture and mix until well blended. Refrigerate dough for 30 minutes.

Preheat oven to 375 degrees. Combine sugar and cinnamon in a small bowl. Form dough into 1-inch balls and roll in sugar-cinnamon mixture. Place 2 inches apart on a baking sheet. Bake about 10 to 12 minutes or until golden brown. Remove and cool on rack.

Makes 2 ½ dozen

APPLE CRISP

8 to 10 medium to large apples (Fuji or Jonathan work well)

⅓ cup orange juice

2 cups flour

2 cups sugar

½ teaspoon salt

¾ teaspoon cinnamon

1 cup butter

Preheat oven to 375 degrees. Core, peel, and slice apples. Spread in the bottom of a 9 x 13-inch glass baking dish. Pour orange juice over the top.

In a large bowl, mix together flour, sugar, salt, and cinnamon. Cut in butter with a pastry blender or two knives until crumbly. Spread over apples and pack down gently.

Bake for 20 to 25 minutes, or until golden brown. Check with fork to make sure apples are tender.

Makes 12 servings

Serve warm with vanilla bean ice cream.

✳ DRINKS ✳

These drink recipes make a nice complement to many of the other recipes in this chapter.

CUCUMBER PUNCH

1 12-ounce can lemonade frozen concentrate

1 12-ounce can limeade frozen concentrate

1 cucumber scored and cut into slices

1 liter ginger ale

1 liter lemon-lime soda (Shasta works best)

Mix lemonade frozen concentrate, limeade frozen concentrate, and cucumber in a punch bowl. Add ginger ale and lemon-lime soda. Then add the amount of water that you normally would add for the lemonade and limeade.

Serve in glasses with ice.

Makes 8 to 12 servings

SWEET ISLAND DRINK

10 ice cubes

1 12-ounce can crushed pineapple with juice

1 14-ounce can unsweetened coconut milk

Put ice cubes in blender and blend on high until crushed. Add pineapple with juice and coconut milk. Blend until smooth. Serve immediately.

Makes 6 servings

POMEGRANATE PUNCH

1 16-ounce bottle pomegranate juice
1 2-liter bottle lemon-lime soda
fresh mint sprigs for garnish (optional)

Combine chilled pomegranate juice and lemon-lime
soda. Serve over ice in glasses or freeze until slushy.
Garnish with fresh mint sprigs if desired.

Makes 16 servings

STRAWBERRY LEMONADE

1 12-ounce can frozen pink lemonade
1 12-ounce package frozen strawberries (with juice and sugar)
fresh strawberries for garnish (optional)

Put frozen lemonade and strawberries, slightly thawed, in a blender and blend. Pour into a large pitcher and add cold water according to directions for lemonade. Serve in tall glasses with ice, garnished with fresh strawberries, if desired.

Makes 6 servings

PALE PARTY PUNCH

1 12-ounce can frozen grapefruit-juice concentrate, thawed
1 12-ounce can frozen lemonade concentrate, thawed
7 cups cold water
4 cups lemon-lime soda

In a 6-quart nonmetal container, combine grapefruit-juice concentrate, lemonade concentrate, and water. Mix well. Refrigerate until well chilled. Just before serving, slowly add lemon-lime soda; stir gently. This drink is quite tart.

Makes 15 servings

CRANBERRY PINEAPPLE PUNCH

2 cups cranberry juice

1 cup pineapple juice

1 cup orange juice

1 4-ounce jar maraschino
   cherries with juice

2 tablespoons lemon juice

1 12-ounce can ginger ale

fresh orange slices for garnish

In a large pitcher, combine cranberry juice, pineapple juice, orange juice, and juice from maraschino cherries; reserve cherries. Add lemon juice. Chill in the refrigerator. Just before serving, slowly add the ginger ale. Serve over ice in glasses (or freeze until slushy and then add ginger ale). Garnish with the maraschino cherries and fresh orange slices.

Makes 8 servings

FAVORS

Favors are a lovely gesture that give guests a memento to remember the shower by. Especially with tiny remembrances, presentation is everything. You can give something as simple as a handful of candies or a tiny magnet, but if it is carefully and creatively packaged it will feel like a little treasure. Use small gift bags, boxes, cellophane, netting, jars, buckets, beautiful or unusual wrapping paper, nametags, and ribbons. Tie up candies in clear cellophane with fancy ribbon, or wrap a bar of specialty soap in thick, beautiful paper with an elaborate gift tag. The packaging should give as much pleasure as the tiny token inside. This chapter offers dozens of ideas for favors to send home with your guests.

○ SWEET TREATS ○

- Jelly Belly candies
- Hershey's Kisses
- Toblerone or Lindt chocolate
- Altoids or any mints in tins
- chocolate-dipped strawberries
- chocolate-dipped pretzels
- boxed sandwich mints
- bottle of Martinelli's Sparkling Cider
- decorated sugar cookies
- small package of Pepperidge Farms cookies
- big 24-ounce candy bar
- candy-covered Jordan almonds

○ BABY YOURSELF, NOT JUST YOUR BABY ○

- slippers or socks
- nail polish
- manicure set
- bath gels or salts
- lotion
- bubble bath
- lip balm
- bracelet

- fancy soaps
- fragrant room spray
- fresh flowers
- herbal teas

○ REMINISCENCES ○

- favorite children's book
- mini book
- picture frame
- note cards
- journal
- candles
- magnets
- small potted plant or herb
- favorite movie on DVD
- music CD
- potpourri
- bookmark with a quote about babies

Great Quotations
ABOUT BABIES

"A baby is God's opinion that life should go on."
                    —Carl Sandburg

"Every baby born into the world is a finer one than the last." —Charles Dickens

"It sometimes happens, even in the best of families, that a baby is born. This is not necessarily cause for alarm. The important thing is to keep your wits about you and borrow some money." —Elinor Goulding Smith

"Babies are always more trouble than you thought—and more wonderful." —Charles Osgood

"Babies are such a nice way to start people."
                    —Don Herrold

"It was the tiniest thing I ever decided to put my whole life into." —Terri Guillemets

"When the first baby laughed for the first time, the laugh broke into a thousand pieces and they all went skipping about, and that was the beginning of fairies."
                    —James M. Barrie

"It is the nature of babies to be in bliss."
                    —Deepak Chopra

"Every baby needs a lap."
                    —Henry Robin

"A baby will make love stronger, days shorter, nights longer, bankroll smaller, home happier, clothes shabbier, the past forgotten, and the future worth living for."
                    —Anonymous

"A baby is born with a need to be loved—and never outgrows it." —Frank A. Clark

DETAILS

When it comes to entertaining, it's surprising how much depends on the details. Whether it's a garnish on a dessert plate or a tiny metal baby bootie tied to the ribbon of a package, the details of your shower are what make it really stand out. Find clever or unusual shower invitations, use interesting greenery in your floral centerpieces, wrap your packages creatively, and search out that perfect little gift for the favors to make your shower special. The details will make the difference between an average party and something to be remembered.

Following are a few suggestions for details you can incorporate into your baby shower:

- Handwrite the addresses on your invitations—don't use labels.
- Write out the directions to your house and include them with your invitation. This is more attractive than including a xeroxed map. Give directions to the guests without their having to ask.
- Line wrapping paper with a layer of tissue paper.
- Choose unusual ribbons and wrapping paper for your gift. Consider wrapping baby presents in fun gift bags, colorful tin buckets, baskets, miniature crates, or other unusual packaging.
- Find a little trinket to tie to the ribbon of your package, such as an ornament, button, soft baby toy, rattle, or miniature picture frame.
- Use china or pottery, glass glasses, and real flat-ware instead of paper plates and plastic silverware.
- Use white linen tablecloths and napkins to dress up your shower.
- Use a punch bowl as your centerpiece. Decorate the base with sprigs of pine boughs, daisies, or fresh cranberries.

- Stand up silverware in a pottery container instead of laying it on the table.
- Find serving dishes that match or contrast nicely. Modern silver platters can complement many styles of dishes.
- Use cake stands to serve desserts or stacks of fruit; they will add height to your buffet table.
- Always use real flowers.

○ IN CONCLUSION ○

A baby shower is a time for joy and celebration. Enjoy the planning, the shopping, the cooking, the gift giving, and all the details. Enjoy honoring the mother-to-be as you join together with family and friends to celebrate the miracle of a new life coming into the world.

About the Author

Jennifer Adams received her degree in English literature from the University of Washington in Seattle. She has hosted dozens of parties and showers for friends, neighbors, coworkers, and family members. Her favorite names for a baby boy are William and Jack. Her favorite names for a baby girl are Abby and Isabel. Jennifer lives with her husband, Virgil Grillone, in Salt Lake City. She is also the author of *Lion House Weddings* and *Wedding Showers,* and the coauthor of *Packing Up a Picnic.*